Eve's Lament

poems by

Heather Corbally Bryant

Finishing Line Press
Georgetown, Kentucky

Eve's Lament

For my children

Copyright © 2018 by Heather Corbally Bryant
ISBN 978-1-63534-386-1 First Edition
All rights reserved under International and Pan-American Copyright Conventions.
No part of this book may be reproduced in any manner whatsoever without written permission from the publisher, except in the case of brief quotations embodied in critical articles and reviews.

ACKNOWLEDGMENTS

"Early in January" was first published in Cheap Grace (Finishing Line Press, 2011)

I would like to thank all my teachers, mentors, friends, colleagues, and students who have listened to my words.

Publisher: Leah Maines

Editor: Christen Kincaid

Cover Art: Rob Houghton

Author Photo: Heidi Lynne Photography

Cover Design: Elizabeth Maines McCleavy

Printed in the USA on acid-free paper.
Order online: www.finishinglinepress.com
also available on amazon.com

Author inquiries and mail orders:
Finishing Line Press
P. O. Box 1626
Georgetown, Kentucky 40324
U. S. A.

Table of Contents

Early in January 1
Exemplary Life 2
Propter Chorum 3
Winter Air 4
My Maternal Grandmother 5
Growing Children 6
Birth Day 7
The Words 8
Still Life 9
Good Night 10
Jewels 11
Disentangling 12
Growing Up 13
What If 14
A Doctor Visit 15
The Huntress 16
Night School 17
Clay Snowman 18
The Divorce of a Friend 19
The Goose 20
What I Know 21
Wash Day 22
Reckoning 23
On Suffering 24
Casting Doubt 25
Night Sky 26
Sparks in the Dark 27
Eve's Lament 28

Early in January

In clear winter light,
All faults are exposed,
As we may rush to flight,
In forests of night—

Still, earth resolves to
Turn, our sun comes up,
Closer now, lower in
The sky, so that rain

May freeze and white stuff
Falls again, while we sculpt
A snowman, complete with
Hat, scarf, carrot nose and

Leftover black buttons,
Talisman of a free afternoon—
All too soon, entire
Childhoods vanish.

Exemplary Life
> *"For a writer there is no such thing as exemplary life"*
> —Tobias Wolff

All impressions come to me rare, raw
Intimate: the universe stretched infinite,
White snow blurring in a blizzard of
Crystals falling downward from the sky,
A fresh page in a notebook, ready to be filled,
Floating with words scribbling across a page:
One red cardinal sitting in a bare apple tree.

Propter Chorum
    —For the sake of the choir

Along the way, each of us discovers
Something slightly different to embrace—
We join this world naked, and newborn—
Same start, at the get-go—then we grow
Our lives as we may, swaying, fighting,
Rejoicing—listening, or not, to some silent,
Private voice we hear, whispering in our
Ears, praying, laughing, cajoling. The pity
Only comes when we think we need to please
Everyone, or anyone; if we can find the way
To a self we know as our own, then may we
Fly, swim, and dance here on earth, with
Whatever days remain for us.

Winter Air

Even the dogs hesitate,
Shaking off frigid breeze,
Pressing tender paws
Against ice, flaking arctic
Grass; everywhere around,
Winds surround, with gusts,
Gales, and grunts, hoping for
A break, we cup our hands
Around mugs, sipping hot
Cocoa and chicken soup,
Being reminded again that
The weather still rules us:
Two old cats shiver under
The porch, flicking their tails
To break up the frozen water.

My Maternal Grandmother

Today you would have turned one
Hundred and six, lit more candles
Than could fit on one birthday cake,
Chocolate it would be, your choice.

You lived long, and hard, writer you
Were, falling just short of that
Centennial that you longed for,
Hoped for, prayed for—but

In the end, as that difficult year
Lurched to a close, you shut your
Eyes and struggled off to another
Land, a place where dark bile and

Bad dreams could melt away and
You could remember how to live
Free and clear, holding close
Pictures of old Shanghai.

Growing Children

So much of what happens seems invisible,
A confluence of body, mind, and spirit
Based on day to day; our presence is
Simply required, expected, accepted until,
Only if it were not here, would it be
Noticed, the small accretion of making a
Life: being around with gladness, joy,
Attending to what happens by the hour.

Birth Day

On a winding road beside new grass,
Blue waters hugging bouldered Nova
Scotia coast, we told you how you were
Made, how life comes about—you
Stared back in wonderment, three sets
Of wide blue eyes,

As we answered your questions,
Pouring forth—we thought back
Ourselves to that hot last day in June
When a doctor said congratulations
Two times over, while I sat in the car—

Waiting until you bought quarts of
Tomato juice, my new sudden craving,
Carrying brown bags through the heat;
Now, ten years later, here you are.

The Words

When I look up from the page,
Almost a whole day has passed;
Sun has crossed the sky, Helios
Having driven his carriage clear
From one side to the other.

Everywhere I peer, I see words
Turning, swirling, twisting upon
Themselves, in beauty and glory,
Simplicity of sound, absorption
In a writing life.

Still Life

Sweet Valencia orange juice, Columbian coffee poured,
Morning sun through clear blue glass, sparrows
Hopping from grass to an old oak tree—
These prosaic offerings belong to the realm of the
Sacred in wintertime; set against the whiteness of snow,
Blanketing our senses, numbing them until we startle
At the extravagantly unexpected beauty of seeing
Something, as if for the very first time.

Good Night

Just one more story turns into three,
My youngest son nestles next to me,
His soft arm curves around mine,
The sound of my own voice almost
Puts me to sleep; he turns, squirms,
Burrows his face into the pillow, lies
Perfectly still; I smooth the covers,
He does not stir until I shift my weight,
Stroke his cheek, place one sweet kiss
On his warm forehead.

Jewels

In a way, it is my curse
To be cast among words,
To rush for a pen crossing
A page, to find a sound
Coming across my fingers,
A magical syllable, flashing
Now, like kingfisher, silver.

Before, I couldn't live on this
Earth, I thought I wasn't
Entitled to be here, that I
Was extra, a bother, sort of like
A half-caste, until you kissed
Me back to life.

And showed me in the realest
Way of all, what matters.

Disentangling

Piece by piece, I detach myself
From you, plucking off your
Touch as I might, like a bird
In flight, I see on a clear winter
Morning how wrong you are—

I never did belong to you, never
Have, never will—that was just a
Fiction which grew in your mind
Until you couldn't bear to tell
Yourself otherwise.

I am not your doll or toy or
Mouthpiece, I don't like what
You like, I don't want to go
Where you do; most of all,
I am realizing that you are

Not my husband anymore, not then,
Not now, not ever; get your
Sharp claws away from me.

Growing Up

As I watch you trudge off to school,
Backpack, mittens, hat, and boots
On this below zero morning, I
Know you are already on your way—

Though you seem to belong to my
Heart and soul, I know it's just a trick
Of time that you are near; if we raise
You right, then you will go where

You will, explore, wonder, and get into
Scrapes here and there, some of your
Own making, some not—like a
Boomerang,

You will arc out into the sky until
Some grace-filled moment when
You will know that it is time again
To make a visit home.

Somewhere along your path to
Adventure, you will stop and find
Your way—and we will wait.

What If

If someone handed me my life,
I wouldn't believe it—instead
I would think there had been a
Mistake made somewhere along
The way; I still think of myself
As a gawking teenager, sitting,
Talking on the phone,
Asking my best friend for advice
While my mother set the table;

Now, I am that woman—
Rushing around, seeing to it
That there is food, clean laundry,
Maybe some chocolate chip
Cookies in the oven somewhere,
Homework started, dinner thought
About, errands run, more left to
Do in the morning: the myriad
Of mosaic pieces which go
Into the making of lives these days.

A Doctor Visit

Just an extra fold on the neck—
There, I see it now, the doctor
Said, pointing her magic wand
Along my belly—but what does
That tell us?

Everything and nothing, so
We understood her to be saying
A thickening here can suggest
So many things gone wrong,
Perhaps an extra chromosome—

So we learned on that warm
August afternoon, we had
Thrown the dice up in the
Air; we held each other close
And decided for life,
Whatever that might mean.

The Huntress

I draw a circle around my body,
Like a shield you say, where
She cannot come in; here is
My life, where the story begins.

I wish it could be otherwise
That we could talk of whatever
It is that wives speak
About to their husbands.

But you want more of me
Than there is to give, more
Than you can take; more than
You ever had a right to ask.

Night School

A seminar table of faces looking
Back at me—expectant, upturned,
A roomful of stories waiting to
Unfold, unfurl, and unravel as they may.

Each with pencil, or pen, paper,
Thoughts on where to begin, perhaps
All over again, as if having
Started school for the first time,
Undoing all that was ever heard before—

Giving themselves one last chance.

Clay Snowman
> *"A mind of winter"*
> —Wallace Stevens

For weeks now, you have talked of baking
Clay, of molding the sticky shapes in your
Hands, of the long wait until they will be
Baked, finally ready to bring home.

Today, your backpack heavy, you trudge
Up our hill, burdens carried inside.
"Look here," you say, unwrapping a
Mound of crushed, taped newspaper.

I pull out a snowman, three-layered,
Round with pointed beak-like nose,
Glazed in a translucent blue.
I put it on the kitchen windowsill—

A creation, just from you, a gift of color
In an otherwise darkened winter.

The Divorce of a Friend

Your face has turned away now,
Harsh with disappointment, sorrow,
Blue eyes narrowed, gaze
Averted, pain too great to let on;

A brown bag with wine inside
June days filled with strawberries,
Lilies, seems so far away now—
Some said then it was an odd union

At best; but still, people always
Hope for what seems difficult—the
Simple fact that being close to
Another human being can be
Near to the impossible.

Here on this wintry morning,
You drive your exuberant daughter
To school, visage ready for world,
Before you go home to cry.

I know I am next.

The Goose
    For SW

Raising your arms in a familiar
Gesture, you exclaim that we are of
The earth; when we leave it, we will
Come back as a part of it, forever,
Everywhere scattered in leaf,
Water, sky—like the goose you
Buried that spring day when
She could no longer fly.

What I Know

What I see, right in front of me,
Is what I know, what matters
Heretofore to take away what
I've been told, to peel back the
Layers to what I know, that is
The essence of writing stories.

All along I understood that
Someone else held one key to
The knowledge room, that there
Was a right answer forever
Unknown, just out of reality;
Now I see: it all belongs to me.

Wash Day

Clean hum of washing machine, spin of the
Dryer, clothes rumpled, dirty, piled on a
Floor, made new again by me, put back
Into drawers, made ready for a new
Experience: it all starts here—what I
See, can do, all over again.

Reckoning

Why do I take the pleasure away?
Tell myself that it cannot stay—
A slope sliding, each day:
Let me see what I can be—
Gray winter morning, sun rise
Over mountains, a veil of cool
Mist on snow—
By noon, brightness falls in
A ring of bones. Years ago,
If you'd told me my fortune,
I would have laughed and said
It couldn't possibly be so.

On Suffering

> *"About suffering they were never wrong, the old masters"*
> —W.H Auden

You receive the new bad news like a
Slice on your hand, a blow to your head;
Too much, really, more than any of us
Should have to bear in our lifetimes.

I don't know what to say—not
Knowing, I wander through a market
On a winter's afternoon; these things
I cull: dried apricots, black chocolates,

Red cyclamen, tangerines; on the way
Home, I decide to make you a pot of
Hot lentil soup; I bring it to you warm,
With bread, to bring you back to the
Living, my dear friend.

Casting Doubt

It's as if you must take away pleasure,
Chipping at it, whack by whack, word
By word—is it that you cannot

Trust in joy, that you will not
Allow it to be—with every new
Adventure, you ask if it must be so—

And yes, I say, yes it must. Or else it won't be so.

Night Sky

All evening we fly—across the world,
Journeying westward past sunset,
Through billowing clouds until
Blackness descends and we cannot
See a single finger in front of our eyes.

We fight the trade winds buffeting the
Globe, earth spins out wide around us,
The universe expands, flattens, surrounds—
Until we awake to first dawn across the
Pacific Ocean; the world turns.

We land on the continent of Oceania and
We lost a day, to be made up on our return.

Sparks in the Dark

If you stop and think too long,
You could get yourself mighty
Discouraged, war, strife,
Famine, man against woman,
Waifs staring, like buffoons we
Climb and tangle and subvert
One another, over and again.

On my darkest days, I
Wonder if it is all just a process
Of moving things from one place
To the other—uselessly, repeating.

No, you say, there is another
Way to look at our existence—at
The magic responsible for getting
Any of us here in the first place.

Sparks in the dark, so we are—
Fireflies on a July evening.

Eve's Lament
> *"Imagination is more important than knowledge."*
> —*Einstein*

You sat and stared in the mirror,
Wishing and wishing someone
Else could be there, that you
Could fill yourself up with
Something that might last—

The waters rippled, and your
Face teetered, shaking in the
Sunshine; I dared to tell you
Some things first, remember,
Like who began the life of sin,
An apple plucked right out of a tree.

Heather Corbally Bryant (formerly Heather Bryant Jordan) teaches in the Writing Program at Wellesley College. Previously, she taught at the Pennsylvania State University, the University of Michigan, and Harvard College where she won awards for her teaching. She received her A.B. with honors in History and Literature from Harvard where she received the Boston Ruskin Prize for her thesis, "Sight and Sensibility: A Study of *Praeterita*." She received her PhD in Modern British and Irish Literature from the University of Michigan where she was a Regents Fellow.

Her academic publications include, *How Will the Heart Endure: Elizabeth Bowen* and *the Landscape of War"* (University of Michigan Press, 1992). This study of the relationship between war and literature was awarded the Donald Murphy Prize for best first book. In addition, she has assisted in the research for the Cornell Yeats Series as well as publishing articles on Bowen, Yeats, O'Faolain, and T.S. Eliot. She has given papers at international conferences and was a plenary speaker at the centennial celebration of Elizabeth Bowen held at University College, Cork.

Beyond her academic publications, Heather Corbally Bryant has published five books of poetry. Finishing Line Press published her first poetry chapbook, *Cheap Grace*, in 2011. In addition, she has published poems in *The Christian Science Monitor* and the 2007 anthology of poetry, *In Other Words*. The Parallel Press Poetry Series of the University of Wisconsin Libraries published *Lottery Ticket*, her second chapbook in 2013. She has given readings at The Pennsylvania State University, The University of Wisconsin at Madison, The University of Illinois at Chicago, Southern Florida University in Ft. Lauderdale, Folio Bookstore, San Francisco the Palmer Art Museum in State College, the Transatlantic Connections Conference in Donegal, Ireland, Wellesley College, the University of Kentucky, Notre Dame, Georgia State, and Harvard College. *Compass Rose*, her third poetry collection, from Finishing Line Press appeared in March 2016. Her first full-length collection of poetry, *My Wedding Dress*, was published by Finishing Line Press in November 2016. Her fifth volume, and second full-length collection, *Thunderstorm*, appeared from the Finishing Line Press in the autumn of 2017. Her work of creative non-fiction, *You Can't Wrap Fire in Paper*, will appear in the spring of 2018 from Arden Writer Press.

www.ingramcontent.com/pod-product-compliance
Lightning Source LLC
LaVergne TN
LVHW041516070426
835507LV00012B/1603